# A Short Biography of Emma Brumm

Written in 1979 by her paperboy Clayton Kauzlaric
*Revised 2025*

# Contents

# About This Story

This biography is a paper I wrote in Junior High – or it was. I grew up in Kitsap County. When I was 11 years old, my family moved out to the Lone Rock area near Seabeck, Washington. A few years later I inherited a paper route from my sister.

The first newspaper I delivered each day was to the house next to the Lone Rock Store. The gate to the front walkway had a sign bearing the name "Bill Brumm," though he had passed away a decade earlier. A lady who lived there asked if I would be willing to walk the paper up to the front porch, knock on the front door and hand the paper to her elderly mother. A couple customers had mobility issues, and I was always happy to take a few extra steps.

I eventually got to know Emma Brumm and her daughter Bertha "Doddie" Sibon. When my Washington State History teacher asked us to interview an elderly person I immediately thought of Emma, who agreed to help. Sadly, she passed away as I was preparing to write, but Doddie saved the day. She lent me notebooks filled with Emma's personal recollections and photographs. She also shared her own stories about her mother.

At 29 pages my report was far longer than required. My teacher was delighted. But no project written by a 15-year-old is going to be perfect. A page of corrections and clarifications Doddie provided went missing when the original document was lent out and copied.

Jumping ahead, stray pages of the original made their way onto Ancestry.com I was amazed that some family trees took the information to heart. Family lore is a wonderful thing, but details are often smoothed over or mixed up through the decades. The stories from Emma were from college essays – No doubt based on real things, but we have no way of knowing how much she dramatized and improvised to tell an entertaining story. I dug up the original paper to fix a number of inaccuracies and some of the cringeworthy teenage prose. Thanks to modern databases, I was also able to verify, expand and correct a few things from the 1979 version. I was also able to incorporate those long-lost notes from Doddie.

The images in my old report were low quality. I paid ten whole cents per page for the copier at the Lone Rock Store before returning the originals to Doddie, who lived right next door. I've done some work to enhance and improve the images. Some pictures have added restoration work using AI enhancement. Great care was taken to not alter faces, clothing and other details of the photos.

I live on the other side of Puget Sound now. Most of my career has been in the tech industry making video games. But revisiting this report brought back strong memories of another time and place. I was once again coasting down Pioneer Road on my old Schwinn to pick up copies of the Bremerton Sun before handing the first copy to Emma. It's been a treat to visit a time and place that gets more remote with each passing year. It's a bit strange to correct my teenage homework, but it was worth the trip.

Clayton Kauzlaric - December 2025

*The cover of the offending document - My school report from 1979, titled "A Neato Bit of Americana."*

2

*Neligh, Nebraska - Early 20th Century*

# Growing Up In Nebraska

Emma F. Bowers was born in Neligh, Nebraska on May 7, 1893. She was the second of six daughters born to Andrew and Magdalena "Lena" Bowers. Both parents were from families of predominantly German descent.

Lena's father was said to be a sea captain who died at sea, leaving her mother Maria to raise Lena, who was eight at the time, with two younger brothers, ages six and four. When Lena was sixteen, her mother decided to leave Germany for America.

They settled in Nebraska at a place called Niobrara, near the border with South Dakota. There, Lena met Andrew Bowers. Andrew was a first-generation son of German immigrants. He was born in Wisconsin but grew up in Iowa in the home of his stepfather. Andrew was 14 years older than Lena and made his living as a general

3

laborer and carpenter. Andrew's granddaughter Bertha would later recall that Lena and her mother saw Andrew as a protector in their adoptive country.

Andrew Bowers (adapted from Bauer) was born in Wisconsin in 1859. He never met his biological father, Leonard. Family lore says that Andrews mother Amelia was pregnant when Leonard Bowers left for gold fields in the West with the intention of sending for his family after he established himself. That never happened – the members of Leonard's wagon train were massacred.

The family legend describes Leonard's dying on his way to the California Gold Rush, but the year given was some time after the gold fields in California were depleted. It's possible Leonard was on his way to the *Colorado* (Pikes Peak) Gold Rush, which was underway in 1859. 1859 was also a year of frequent conflicts between settlers and native tribes in Nebraska and Colorado, though the name "Leonard Bowers" doesn't appear in contemporary records or newspapers of known attacks.

There is clearly more to the story than  we can easily discover after 160 years. A missing husband wasn't unusual during the era. Stories of meeting a dramatic death were also a common way to give a single mother a bit of respectability. It's telling that in 1860 Amelia and her infant son Andrew lived under her maiden name in Burlington, Wisconsin. She is listed as a servant in the home of James Catton – an industrialist friend of Amelia's brother-in-law, Henry Trowbridge. Catton and Trowbridge served in government roles together for years. If Amelia were widowed, not using her married name is a curious choice. Living outside her family home and that of the Bowers is also noteworthy. When Amelia's mother moved to Iowa to run a boarding house a few years later she and Andrew went with her, now using the Bowers name. Amelia would later tell stories to her grandchildren, one of which Emma recalled in a college paper:

*One day some Indians came filing into grandmother's home. Indians never knocked, they just opened the door and walked in. These Indians, at first, did not seem to want anything in particular. They went about fingering various things and finally asked for bread in guttural voices.*

*My grandmother was alone at the time and was dreadfully frightened. She knew, however, that Indians admired courage, so she managed in some way to sing and pretend that she was unafraid.*

*When the Indians finished eating, the leader of the band sauntered over to the crib, where the baby who later became my father lay sleeping. My grandmother was afraid that he meant to harm the child and grabbed the knife she had used to cut the bread and rushed to her baby's side."*

*The old chief chuckled and said, 'Heap brave squaw! No hurt papoose!' and calling the other Indians, he left the house.*

*He returned later, carrying over his arm two beautiful, red woolen blankets, which he presented to my grandmother. These blankets later became my mother's and their appearance to strangers always called for the telling of the story connected with them.*

It's very possible Emma and her grandmother embellished the tale to add a touch of drama, which may have grown with each retelling.

When Andrew was six, Amelia married a man named Jacob A. Ommen. One of Amelia's sisters was married to Jacob's brother Peter, so it's likely the two met through gatherings of the Hartmann and Ommen families. Jacob was a postmaster, carpenter and teamster. He became the only father figure in Andrew's life, and the only grandfather Andrew's children ever knew.

Jacob and Amelia followed the Bowers to Neligh, Nebraska during the 1890s. Jacob ran a hauling business with his wagon and team of horses and was well-regarded in his church and community. A favorite pastime was accompanying his wife on his violin as she sang hymns. The couple were in increasingly poor health after 1900. Amelia died in 1902 and Jacob came to live with Andrew and Lena's family. Emma wrote fondly of him years later:

> *I have never known a dearer, kinder man than he was. Although blinded by the falling of a heavy beam upon his head when he was only about thirty-two years old, his blindness seemed only to make him more tender.*
>
> *After my grandmother's death, he came to live with us, and our years of contact with him have served to make us kinder to all blind persons.*
>
> *Grandfather lived with us until he was seventy-six years old. Through all his blind years his violin was his constant companion. He loved to play hymns and also improvised beautiful waltz music. When his fingers became too stiff to handle the strings properly, he seemed to lose all interest in life, and I remember the day when he laid aside his beloved instrument and prayed God to soon take him home. He was a deeply religious man.*

Jacob's final years weren't easy for the Bowers family. Andrew and Lena had five daughters when Jacob came to live with them. Their eldest daughter Matie died that year at the age of eleven after an illness lasting several weeks. Another daughter was born in 1903. The family struggled to look after Jacob while supporting a growing family. He was incoherent at times and required constant supervision.

The situation didn't go unnoticed by a local newspaper. Ommen, it was noted, "has knocked the stove pipe down once or twice, and, in various ways we cannot mention here, is such a care that Mrs. Bowers is nearly worn out." The burden this placed on Andrew was also concerning. "Andy needs all his time working to support his large family but has been obliged to stay home a good deal to look after the failing invalid."

It was proposed that the community take action to help care for Ommen and give the Bowers some relief. Before that could happen, Jacob Ommen died in 1904.

*Andrew and Lena Bowers, early 1920s.*

The first things Emma Bowers could recall of her own life started one September when she was a little over four years old, around the time Emma's parents moved the family from Neligh to a small farm in Oakdale, Nebraska.

Her older sister was starting school and Emma, though too young to go to school, cried and pleaded to be allowed to go with her sister. Her mother finally consented, and the two sisters went off to the schoolhouse. The school was small, and the teacher didn't mind if young Emma remained with the other children.

Emma couldn't recall whether she learned anything at the school or what sort of work she did, but she remembered classic nineteenth century schoolhouse pranks like the older boys putting the girl's pigtails into inkwells or snipping off the ends of braids with their pocketknives.

The school's teacher was replaced by a man the following year. He was less enthused about Emma tagging along with her sister but was willing to allow it. That ended when a bored Emma wet her finger and poked holes through every large "O" in an eighth-grade geography textbook.

"Needless to say, I went home in disgrace," she said later.

The following year, the Bower family moved back to Neligh. Emma was now old enough to attend school on a more official basis but first moved into the home of a woman named Mabel Boyd, the wife of a local politician. Reflecting later, she wrote:

> *One evening, when I was about eleven years old, my father came home from work and startled us all by saying, "Which one of you youngsters wants a job?" There were five of us in the family, all girls, and up to this time the idea of getting a job had never entered our minds. We had been content to just play around during vacation time and through the rest of the year schoolwork kept*

*us occupied, as mother always demanded good report cards. It never entered our heads to even think of lying down on the job when it came to our studies.*

*Being the oldest child, when father spoke all eyes were turned toward me, and of course I said, "I do!"*

*Father then told us that Mrs. Boyd, a lady for whom he had worked that day, wanted a schoolgirl to stay with her while her husband, who was waging a campaign for congressman, was away from home.*

The woman offering the job was Mabel Boyd. Her husband was John F. Boyd. Boyd was a local politician who had served as a sheriff and district court judge in Antelope County. He won a congressional seat in 1906 and represented Nebraska's 3rd Congressional District from 1907 to 1909. Emma went to work in the Boyd household years before then but John Boyd's job as a circuit judge sometimes took him to remote corners of the state. It makes sense that Mabel Boyd may have needed extra help or company around the house.

Emma's departure caused great excitement within the Bowers home.

*After some deliberation, it was decided that I should go to the Boyd's, whose home, a big three-storied house, seemed almost a palace beside our little six room cottage.*

*Such a scurrying as there was to get me ready! Everybody wanted to do something for me, and it seemed as if I were going to China, or some other equally distant place, instead of only about a mile and a half away.*

*'You can take my new red ribbon' said my sister Mary.*

9

*John F. Boyd*

'You can take my comb and brush set; they're nicer than yours," said another sister.

I seemed they all wanted to be nice to me, even Josephine, with whom I had quarreled a few minutes before.

In the morning my father took me with him when he went to work, and I remember how my heart thumped, until I could hear it, when we walked up the steps and rang the doorbell.

Mrs. Boyd, a beautiful, sweet-faced, white-haired lady, opened the door, invited us in, and seated us in a sort of reception hall which had comfortable wall seats, a small fancy table, an umbrella and hat rack, and other small articles of furniture. A polished, shiny, winding stair led to the floor *above, and I remember the thought entering my mind, 'Wouldn't it be fun to slide down the banister?' However, I sat stiffly on the edge of my chair, after Father had told Mrs. Boyd my name, and waited patiently for them to finish their conversation.*

*Father soon left, and I was taken to my room. What a bright, cheerful room it was! And how grown up I felt. Just think! A bureau which need not be shared with anyone, and a bed which folded up in the daytime, making room into a sitting room rather than a bedroom.*

*I put away my clothing and other belongings, and when I could no longer invent any reasons for staying in my room, went downstairs. Once outside my own room, the grown up feeling left me, and I felt very much like just a little girl.*

*Mrs. Boyd was in the library stroking a big, black, tomcat, whose name was 'Tommy-lum.' The cat, a friendly sort of fellow, broke the ice, so to speak, for I also loved cats, and it gave us something to talk about.*

*I managed to get through the morning rather well, Mrs. Boyd giving me a few small tasks to do.*

*When lunch time came, she prepared food and arranged the table. I sort of dreaded the thought of eating, for I feared I should make some blunder in table manners. The meal was a simple one, and I would have gotten along nicely had it not been for the olives. I like olives very much now, but at that time I had never eaten any of them. Mrs. Boyd asked me if I would like some olives, and not wishing to appear dumb by saying that I had never eaten any, I replied, 'Yes please.'*

11

*I seemed to have a premonition that all was not well, and that first bite – I thought I would choke before I got it down – but I managed to eat those two olives somewhat, although each bite seemed likely to be the last that I should be able to take.*

*Long afterward Mrs. Boyd told me that she knew what a terrible time I was having with those olives. She was having nearly as bad a time trying to keep from laughing at me, and there I sat, feeling secure in the knowledge she would never know that I hadn't eaten olives before.*

*When I was about twelve years old, a girl who worked for Mrs. Boyd's friends made some very nice home-made bread. Mrs. Boyd asked if I should like to try to make some, and of course I said I should, and she obtained the recipe from her friend.*

*The first time I followed the recipe exactly, and the result was three nice loaves of bread, for which I was duly praised. This sort of went to my head; the next time I thought I could make bread without the recipe.*

*I set the yeast before I went to bed, and the next morning, it being all bubbly and light, I proceeded to mix the other ingredients. I did not measure the milk, and it seemed to me it took a great deal of flour to make it of the right consistency. Finally, it was done to my satisfaction, and I put it near the radiator to rise. It rose up above my wildest expectations! In a little while it was out over the edge of the pan. What should I do! What could I do? I felt that I must get rid of some of that dough before Mrs. Boyd came downstairs.*

*Searching about frantically for a hiding place, I saw an old, abandoned outhouse in*

*the alley. I didn't even know who it belonged
to, but pinching off a large piece of the bread
dough, I hurriedly carried it out there and
flung it inside. I closed the door tightly and
turned to go back to the house. Mrs. Boyd's
room was on the other side of the house, but
it seemed to me that every window on this
side had accusing eyes peering out at me.*

*My peace of mind was shattered for many
days by my guilty conscience, and each
morning, when I got up, I was almost afraid
to look toward that old building for fear the
bread dough would be pushing its way out
of every crack and crevice.*

*I never went near that building again. I
do not know what became of the dough, but
needless to say, I never made bread without
a recipe again until I was in a home of my
own.*

Emma lived in the Boyd household until she was seventeen. By then, her mother, father and sisters had begun working as household staff for a farmer named Henry Peterson. Emma was being courted by a young man she'd known for years named Bill Brumm. Emma and Bill wanted to marry, but her father insisted the couple wait until after she turned eighteen.

It had been Emma's ambition to become a teacher, likely since following her sister to school. She attended Nebraska State Normal School – now Nebraska State Teacher's College – and received her teaching certificate in 1910. Her goal of becoming a teacher was realized quickly. She was hired that year to teach at a one-room schoolhouse in Randolph, Nebraska.

William "Bill" Brumm was the son of Adolph and Augusta Brumm. His father was a stone mason who was born in a town near the border with Poland. The town was called Birnbaum by its German residents and is now part of Poland. Adolph's parents were German and Polish. Bill was one of nine children born to Adolph and Augusta but only three – Bill and his brothers Carl and Edward – survived to adulthood.

The Brumm family settled and farmed in West Point, Nebraska, where Bill was born in 1888. In 1901, Adolph's tuberculosis prompted the family to seek a healthier climate in Colorado. The family briefly moved back to Nebraska and lived in Neligh, which is likely when Bill met Emma.

During the year Emma attended Normal School and taught in Wayne County, her fiancé Bill went to live with family members on a farm in Milk Creek, Oregon. Many members of the Brumm and Bowers families would settle permanently in the Pacific Northwest.

*Seated: (left) Bill Brumm - (right) Emma*
*Brumm, taken when they married in 1911.*

*Above:The main building of Nebraska Normal School.*

*Right: Emma's first teacher's certificate.*

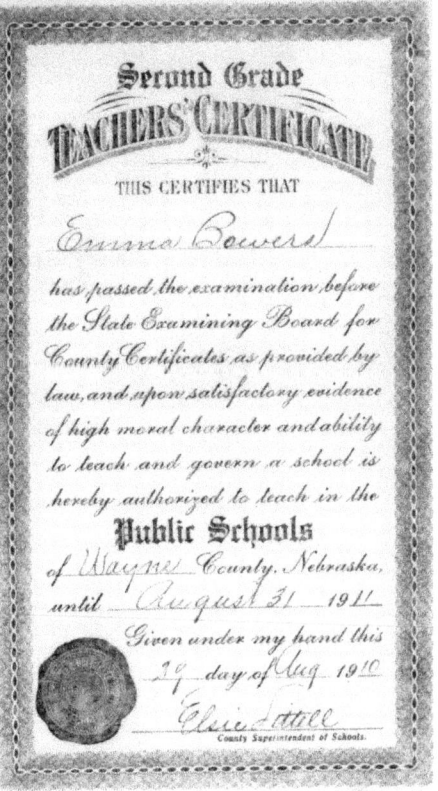

15

*Emma's first teaching contract, 1910.*

Emma's experience as a teacher in 1910 was a stark contrast to the profession of today. Her monthly pay was $45. Her duties included keeping the schoolhouse "in good repair," "janitor work," and providing fuel for the stove that heated the building. The Wayne County School District crossed out the janitorial task on her contract, but Emma found herself doing the work regardless. She arrived some mornings to find that vagrants had camped in the schoolhouse overnight. There were no difficulties resulting from these visits, but the teenage schoolteacher was afraid she might encounter one of the men who had camped at the Neligh school for the night.

Her first class consisted of thirty-three children, ranging through all grades. The demands of farm life meant some of the male students only attended school during the winter months. This meant that some of Emma's students were both older and bigger than her.

She stayed at a boarding house during her first year of teaching. With her limited means, Emma could only afford the most basic lodgings. The lunch they provided for her day at school consisted only of bread and lard. Breakfast and dinner at the boarding house were bread and honey. Emma was relieved when the year was over. She turned 18 and was now free to marry Bill Brumm.

*Above:Bill Brumm (right), working at a Nebraska rail yard, September, 1915.*

*Left: Bill (center/left)supervising a work crew, Nebraska, November 2nd, 1915.*

Bill returned to Nebraska and married Emma in 1911. He worked for a railroad as a section foreman. Emma paused her teaching career after her marriage. She and Bill had three daughters over the next few years. Bertha was born in 1912, followed by Marie Thelma in 1914 and Clare Lena in 1915. The family lived in the eastern end of the state near Bill's family, who had returned to West Point, Nebraska, though railroad work often took the family to other parts of the state.

*Two photos of Bertha "Doddie" Brumm (left, seated in chair and baby carriage) and Emma's youngest sister Helen Bowers (right), Nebraska 1913.*

# Goldendale, Washington

The cities and states of the West were growing quickly. It was a common practice for one family member to move into the region and pave the way for more family members to follow suit. The Brumm family was already putting down roots in the Pacific Northwest during their time in Oregon. Bill's uncle Charles found work at a logging operation near Goldendale, Washington. Letters home encouraged Bill to bring his family, speaking of plentiful work and opportunities. Bill and Emma made the move in 1918 and were joined over the years that followed by a steady stream of friends, siblings, cousins and other family members.

Bill, Emma and their three daughters made the 1500-mile trip by train. While in transit Emma was concerned about her second oldest daughter, Marie Thelma. The child was often unwell and no amount of attention from her mother seemed to soothe the child when she cried. The train trip had not gone well, and Marie Thelma was inconsolable again. A railroad porter stopped at their seat and kindly offered Marie an orange – still a relatively rare treat – hoping it might help calm the child. The porter's efforts had the opposite effect. Marie had never seen a black person and became more hysterical.

In Goldendale, they lived in Orchard Heights. Bertha was only five, but – like her mother – begged to be allowed to go to school. Emma agreed. To prove she was ready to join the older children Bertha tried to impress Emma with her reading skills. She memorized a page in a book and pretended to read it but neglected to hold the book the right-side up. She was quickly removed from school by her mother.

Bertha later recalled a first-grade teacher at Orchard Heights who was dating an aviator. Any time she heard a plane flying overhead she would dismiss her class for the day.

The timber industry was always hazardous. Bill worked as a faller and as a bucker – Jobs that entailed cutting down trees and cutting them with a buck saw into sections suitable for transport. On his World War I draft registration card it's noted that Bill had lost the index finger on his left hand. As a father with dependents Bill was exempted by Goldendale's draft board.

*Buckers prepping tree sections for transport and milling.*
*Brennan, WA, 1905*

In Eastern Washington the weather was often too warm for outdoor picnics during the Summer. Next to the school where Emma taught was a place called the Arbor House, a long gazebo-like structure. One memory that remained with Emma's daughters years later was the excitement that went with the many events held at the structure. Men would go into the hills and return with piles of tree branches. These would be laced through the ceiling beams of Arbor House, transforming it into an "indoor forest" for picnics, parties and civic celebrations.

In 1920, a school in the hills near Goldendale was in danger of closing as only one boy lived in the vicinity. He was joined by another boy, which was considered enough to operate the school provided a teacher could be found. Emma took the job and taught at the small schoolhouse. Her three daughters joined, bringing the student headcount to five for that year. Clara was only five but followed the family tradition of joining her older sisters. Bertha recalled Clara, holding the tail of a dog to keep up with her sisters on the hilly 3-mile walk to school.

After three years in Goldendale Bill's uncle Charles encouraged another move, this time to a logging community in Kitsap County. Again, a network of family and friends from Nebraska and Goldendale would follow suit.

*(left to right) Bill Brumm, his nephew Emil Brumm, and brother Carl Brumm operating a belt-driven saw, Goldendale, WA 1915*

*Postcard of a ferry crossing the Dalles, early 1900s. The Brumm family crossed in a similar vessel with their Model A Ford in 1921.*

# Coming To Kitsap

The destination was the Crosby community in Kitsap County in 1921 where Bill's uncle and his family already lived. Bill Brumm owned one of the first Model A Fords in Goldendale. That car would take his family to their new home. The journey included a memorable crossing at the Dalles on its raft-like barge and a visit to Emma's grandmother Lena Bowers in St. Helens, Oregon. From there, they headed north to their new home.

The headlamps of the car were both electric and kerosene. Light from the kerosene flame was extremely dim. The electric light wasn't much better, growing brighter or dimmer based on the speed of the car. The roads crisscrossing the state will still mostly dirt or gravel with poor signage. To avoid the hazard that presented the family slept in the car each night and continued their journey during daylight hours.

The waters of Puget Sound impressed the Brumms. They'd lived most of their lives in Nebraska. Their years in Goldendale brought them to the Columbia River, but Puget Sound and Hood Canal seemed like unbelievably vast amounts of open water to the Midwesterners.

Instead of improving, the roadways only grew worse as they entered Kitsap County. Bertha later described the roads near Port Orchard as "like a cattle trail," with deep holes and ruts. The city of Bremerton had better roads, but the family had no idea how much further it was to the mill at Crosby. It must have been a welcome change from sleeping in the car when they opted to stay at a hotel on Bremerton's Front Street before continuing their drive to Crosby the next morning.

*The road between Lone Rock and Seabeck, 1920s. The log watering trough was a well-known landmark at the time.*

Crosby was roughly 20 miles west of Bremerton. The Brumm's winding route took them to the shores of Hood Canal and through Seabeck. Seabeck's lumber mill had been the economic hub of the area until it burned in 1886. Remnants of the structure, and pilings were still visible on the shoreline 35 years later as the Brumm's car trundled past. Seabeck's boom years were in the past, but logging and mill work in the surrounding communities were experiencing a resurgence in the 1920s, including Crosby and Camp Union.

The Brumm family lived through the Summer of 1921 with Bill's uncle and his family at a house built by Thomas J. Lewis, one of the early settlers in the area.

*The Brumm daughters (left to right) Marie, Claire and Doddie at Camp Union, 1921. The location was also known as "West Forks."*

When the school year started that Fall, Emma, Bill and their three daughters moved to a place called the Sisoon house near Lone Rock. The house was a Summer residence, and was cold and drafty as Fall weather set in. Emma found teaching work again at Lone Rock School. The first time Emma saw the schoolhouse in 1921 was the subject of a paper called "The Old Schoolhouse," written years later.

> *She left her car at the bend of the road and walked up the trail to the top of the hill.*
>
> *What a beautiful setting for a schoolhouse, high upon a hill where the air was clear and pure. Below, she sees the sparkling, blue waters of Hood Canal, and beyond towers the peaks of the Olympics, the steadfast*

*Constance, The Brothers and many others. Rhododendrons grow in profusion all about the grounds, and giant firs reach toward the sky, standing like sentinels on guard over something precious.*

*Two or three little squirrels stop their work of scurrying back and forth with food for their winter storehouse to gaze at her out of curious, round, frightened eyes. A blue jay in a nearby tree saucily scolds, trying to make up his mind if the intruder is a friend or an enemy.*

*Here is the schoolhouse itself, a small white and green building of one room. See the flowers there by the step, bright marigolds, snowy daisies and blue forget-me-nots. They wave gently in the breeze as if nodding a welcome to all who stop to look at them.*

*She climbs the steps, worn low in the middle by the feet of many happy children. The clerk opens the door and the girl enters. She finds a room about thirty feet long and fifteen feet wide, whose buff and brown walls are gaily decorated with posters and drawings made by the children that went to school here last year. A statue of Lincoln stands in the corner, and it seems as if a feeling of peace and serenity pervade the place.*

*Some of the desks are of the old double kind, liberally decorated with initials and various other designs. Some of these were made by boys and girls who are now gray-haired men and women. There are old recitation benches. How much happiness and how many heartaches these four walls must have held! How many romances had their beginnings in this very room.*

*Left: Carolyn Merrick, photographed on the day of her death, April 23, 1935*

*Below: A recommendation letter written by Merrick for Emma Brumm.*

*"Mrs. Brumm is a natural teacher. She loves her work and her pupils love her. She taught the Lone Rock School for five years and graduated four classes from the eighth grade - We hope you will consider her application favorably."*

To whom it may concern,-

Mrs Brumm is a natural teacher, she loves her work and her pupils love her. She taught the Lone Rock School for five years and graduated four classes from the eighth grade — We hope you will consider her application favorably.

Carolyn E. Merrick
District Clerk

*Many books were in orderly rows on shelves and in cupboards and a set of beautifully bound World Books occupied a conspicuous place.*

*'How many children attend the school here?' the girl asked of the school clerk.*

*'About twenty-five,' replied the man, 'but sometimes we have nearly thirty.'*

*'I believe I shall take the school,' said the young teacher, 'I think that I shall be very happy here.'*

*As she went down the trail the squirrels chattered to one another, 'We're going to like her. She'll be our friend,' and the blue jay flew from tree to tree telling the news to all the feathered friends who might be listening.*

At the end of the 1921-1922 school year, the Brumms moved into a house across Big Beef lagoon from the Sisoon house. The new house was unfinished but a much more comfortable place than their drafty former residence. The property was originally part of three homestead segments first platted by James Robert Smith, with a down payment of $4.51. The Brumm's house and half acre lot were purchased for $450.00. Across the road, Smith had grafted a hawthorn tree that bloomed every year with blossoms that were half pink and half white.

Carolyn Merrick was head clerk at the Lone Rock School. Her duties were varied, including managing teachers, responding to complaints from parents, signing pay vouchers and conducting the final exam for eighth graders. Passing eighth grade was required to move on to high school and would be the last grade for many students at the time.

The local logging industry meant that Lone Rock contained a large number of bachelors. The Brumm family became acquainted with three who lived in a row of cabins near the Sisoon house, coincidentally named Mr. Fox, Mr. Wolfe and Mr. Bear.

One memorable man lived near the delta of the Big Beef river was Herbert B. Creel. Creel was 61 years old and had listed his profession over the decades as a preacher, butcher and would-be politician. He moved with his wife and five children to Spokane in 1900 but was divorced soon after that for lack of support. Creel had an ever-changing list of jobs and lodgings before arriving in Lone Rock.

He was a big man, standing six foot four inches. Creel's political ambitions meant he frequently practiced for speaking engagements with his loud, booming voice. He lived, appropriately enough, on Echo Valley road, which ran past the Lone Rock School on the opposite side of the Big Beef estuary from the Brumm house. Most of the timber had been cleared from the area and his voice could be heard clearly across the hundreds of yards between the two homes.

He was a frequent visitor to the Brumm household and an enthusiastic dinner guest. Creel's table manners were a constant source of entertainment for the three Brumm daughters. He would fashion mashed potatoes into a small mountain, mix in all his peas and shovel the largest possible dollop he could fit into his mouth with a knife. His large mouth, containing two teeth, only added to the spectacle and barely suppressed giggles from the Brumm girls.

Creel often volunteered at the Lone Rock school. He owned an old peddlers wagon that was used to take Lone Rock students to Silverdale for spelling bees and baseball games. Students were forced to get out of the wagon and walk when Creel's wagon made its way up Anderson Hill – then called Day Hill.

Emma taught at the Lone Rock school until 1926. After that, she taught at other schools in the district. She taught at Chico Elementary briefly before working for three years at the Franklin School in Poulsbo, which later became the site of North Kitsap Highschool. The distance from Seabeck made commuting impractical, so Emma stayed at a boarding house while she worked there. Her youngest daughter Clara went with her during those years and attended the school.

Two of Emma's students at Poulsbo went on to careers with the school district. Howard Kvinsland became principal at Chico Elementary. His brother, Stan Kvinsland, was a school principal in Port Orchard.

*Emma with her students at the Franklin School in Poulsbo, 1927*

Emma returned to the Lone Rock school in 1932. The Great Depression had set in. Lone Rock had some benefits during the lean times of the Depression. Residents who lived through the era felt hunger was less of a threat than it was for many Americans. Fruit from orchards, vegetable gardens, wild berries, shellfish from the beach and fish from Hood Canal were lifelines that kept many residents fed when money was tight.

*Emma and the students of Lone Rock School, 1932.*

Bootlegging and smuggling liquor was also a common way to make extra money during the hard times, and the Lone Rock area was no exception. A barn across the road from the Brumm house belonged to a man named Fred Miller. It was generally known that Miller used it to store contraband liquor he brought down from Canada or from rendezvous points to the north using his speed launch. Local law enforcement and Prohibition agents were often paid off and happy to turn a blind eye. According to Doddie Brumm, Miller's delivery method consisted of sinking deliveries at points along the shoreline during high tide, so the intended recipients could retrieve the cases when the tide went out. Some deliveries did go astray on occasion. Brumm girls would sometimes find a case of liquor while beachcombing, which they happily took home.

Family life in Lone Rock centered around the school during the holidays. Each student, even the smallest and shyest, had some part in the annual Christmas program.

*The front yard of the Brumm home, early 1950s.*

The children's parts fit their abilities. Some recited lines while others simple held up artwork or cards that said, "Merry Christmas." A favorite activity was a grab-bag that ensured every person there received a present. It was a source of laughter one year when a local bachelor drew a wedding ring from the bag.

Another neighborhood hub would belong to the Brumm family. Bill stopped working in logging and opened a gas and grocery store next to the family residence at Lone Rock in 1937. With the distance between sources of fuel or groceries requiring a drive to Seabeck or Silverdale, the business became a fixture of the Lone Rock community. Bill's salty, gregarious personality only added to the store's charm.

Bremerton Sun reporter Adele Ferguson described Bill's lively relationship with his customers in 1946.

> *Speaking of people who are really something, there is one man who lives at Lone Rock who is a great influence on the people around there. His name is Bill Brumm and he operates the Lone Rock store. Bill grum-*

31

*bles quite a bit but many mornings he has arisen shortly after dawn to give some early bird some gasoline and oil. All the kids in the neighborhood call him Bill, and what he calls their mothers shocks many a newcomer.*

*"Come on you old battle-axe," he roars at the housewives who shop there. He tells them when they begin to take weight, how they look when they are tramping out in the woods. His store is a small one, but it is the headquarters for everything out there. All the latest gossip may be secured, not from Bill, but from his customers. He knows all events, past, present and future, but he tells nothing.*

*And when the food shortages were on (during WWII), he used to cuss about the people who would come out from town, hoping to find some scarce item in the little store. He refused to sell them and saved his products for his steady customers. When he got a shipment of bananas, he apportioned them according to the sizes of the families – and he knew the sizes.*

*There are many Brumms out at Lone Rock, but Bill is the chief of the clan.*

Bill sold the store in 1950. The community was shocked two years later when the store was destroyed by a fire. Bill, Emma, a crowd of neighbors and the store's new owner watched helplessly as fire consumed the business. The store was rebuilt and reopened. It would see a series of openings, closings and remodels with a series of different owners over the decades that followed.

The loss of the store wasn't the only event impacting Lone Rock in 1952. The Lone Rock and Seabeck School merged in 1952. Many in the Lone Rock community weren't happy to see their local school closed and their children sent miles away to attend Seabeck Elementary.

The schoolhouse had been a source of identity and cohesion for the community.

Emma sometimes served as principal at the Lone Rock school, but the move to Seabeck meant assuming the role of head teacher. The apparent demotion didn't bother her. Bertha later recalled that her mother maintained a belief that school principals should be men, despite Kitsap Schools having a long tradition of women in leadership positions. Emma taught 5th or 6th grade classes during her tenure at Seabeck.

*Emma and her 5th grade class at Seabeck School, 1947.*

The newly merged schools were soon straining the capacity at Seabeck's 1925 two-room schoolhouse. By 1955, the school day was split into an early and a late shift. Grades 4, 5 and 6 attended from 8:AM to noon. Grades 1, 2 and 3 took the second shift, from noon to 4:PM.

A bond had passed in 1954, allocating funds for new elementary schools at Seabeck, Tracyton and Brownsville. When construction began on the new school, Seabeck's old structure was transported by barge and became a community church – directly across a street from Brownsville Elementary. Seabeck's students were bused to schools in Chico and Silverdale during construction.

*Emma's 6th grade class at Seabeck, 1954*

A modern, new school opened in 1956, with Emma teaching 5th grade. In a shocking turn of events, the $234,000 building was completely destroyed in a fire four months later in January of 1957. State legislators investigating the fire theorized that the building may have lacked sufficient a water supply, and adequate water pressure to fight the blaze and made a number of recommendations for future construction projects. The initial cause of the fire itself was never determined.

The building was insured and construction of a replacement was soon underway. The students from Seabeck were again bused to Silverdale and Chico Elementary. The faculty was dispersed to those schools as well, including Emma. The new building was expected to be finished in time for the next school year, but construction delays pushed Seabeck's reopening to February of 1958.

School officials were quick to highlight the plentiful supply of fire extinguishers in newspaper stories.

Emma's long career as a teacher ended in 1960. Friends, colleagues and many of her former students attended a retirement tea at Seabeck Elementary. Emma and Bill celebrated their 50th wedding anniversary in 1961. The couple traveled, enjoying visits with their children and grandchildren and trips to see Emma's family in Oregon.

*Bremerton Sun coverage of the fire at Seabeck Elementary, 1957.*

*Emma and Bill at the Peterson Rock Garden, Oregon, 1956*

Bill Brumm died in 1968. According to his granddaughter Doddie, Bill was doing yard work and sat down to rest for a moment on the porch. He passed away a moment later.

Emma continued to live at the house by the Lone Rock store. She was later joined by her daughter Doddie who cared for her mother in her later years. Doddie described her mother's last moments as well. She woke up as usual on the morning of March 18, 1979. She was sitting on the edge of her bed before starting her day and said, "Oh Doddie... I'm so tired I could sleep all day." With that, Emma lay back on her bed and, like her husband, passed away very quickly.

It's hard to sum up the legacy of someone who taught countless children for so many years, spanning two World Wars, the Great Depression and the dawn of the Space Age. Despite the many changes, both social and technological, there is a consistent thread running through the story of Emma Brumm: her devotion to teaching and her students. The words of Kitsap journalist and chronicler Adele Ferguson, written the year Emma retired say it best:

> *She'll soon close the door forever on the smell of books as only teachers and librarians know it, of chalk dust and pencil erasers, or orange peelings and peanut butter, the sweet smell of the oil the janitor uses on the floor when he sweeps in the still of the evening, of wet coats, ground up shavings in the pencil sharpener, the earthy smell of little boys and the sweet soapy smell of little girls, the overpowering fragrance of lilacs and the inevitable apples.*